As always, this book is dedicated to the thousands of seniors sharing their wit and wisdom within the pages, that have made these books possible. At the end of the book, there is a special section to thank those brave souls by name.

I want to thank my husband Brian, for supporting this writing venture, and all of the chaos that goes with it. They say everyone has that person, who makes life worth living, gives you joy, laughter, small bouts of insanity, aggravation, and hysterical stories to share. That is my Brian-HE IS MY PERSON.

There is no one I would rather share this ride through life with. I love you. That is all.

Foreword

Here we are again, ready to share more of the wit and wisdom that makes us a unique little village of Sarcastic Seniors.

My how we have grown! At the publishing of our first book, we had approximately 12000 Sarcastic Seniors. The second book had us picking the brains of approximately 22000 of the wise ones. Here we are 26 months after that first book, and we are now 47000+ strong.

I have truly enjoyed putting to paper all of the hysterical, worldly, observant, wise, and even the wise-ass tidbits you share with the world.

I want this book to be not only a memoir of our time together, but also a testament to what we have experienced, learned, witnessed, and endured in our lives. We are the generation with the greatest changes in our lives, and we have a lot to share with the younger generations. I think too often, we are 'dismissed', and assumed unimportant in today's fast-paced technological world. That couldn't be further from the truth.

It is from the mistakes, trials, and tribulations in our lives, that we have gained the wealth of knowledge, and good ole common sense, that is often lacking in today's society.

This book is the last in the series. After the completion of this book, I will be taking time off to work on my first novel, something that has been on the 'Lisa-Do' list for a long time. But we will continue hanging out together on the Sarcastic Seniors- this I promise, as I don't think I could do without you wonderful folks.

As always there will be a special dedication are in the back of this book, where I will properly thank all of you brave enough to share your names.

So, let's get ready to spit out our dentures, pee our pants, and share some good ole fashioned belly laughs. Welcome to **"The Sarcastic Seniors- What the Hell Do We Know?**

The Common Thread- The Junk Drawer

We all muddle through life making our way and traveling our road. We may belong to different social circles, and live within different income brackets, but there are many things that we as seniors, and members of this human race, have in common.

Take the junk drawer. We all have one. Many of us have several. This is the place we put those things we don't need now, but may need again, and have no other place to put.

As I always do, I turned this topic over to our Beloved Seniors and asked them to share their thoughts and experiences with the junk drawer fad. They never fail to amuse, enlighten, and entertain. Enjoy!

(Note- In each chapter, I will separate each contributor's comments by making every other one bold, so it is easier to read. And, they are all italicized.)

Having recently cleared out my in-laws' house I can honestly say they were hoarders of the first degree, having over 50 bars of soap is one example and much much more!

I have laid down the law at our new retirement home! Worked 45 years in a furniture factory, got a nice 401k, got a new place in the country, no heavy tools in the kitchen drawers! At the old house, tools kept mysteriously appearing in the kitchen drawers until they all fell! Top on the second drawer, second on the third drawer, then fourth, stacked like pancakes, no more! Use the toolbox or the tools are going in his underwear drawer!

I seriously downsized several years ago, so I don't have a junk drawer per se. At the moment, I am in danger of a junk room. I keep seeing all of these lovely artsy projects I would like to try.

Buttons! I keep every button from old discarded shirts, the "extra" button or two you get with new garments, and every button ever.

**Instead of a drawer, I have a whole extra
bedroom ... I call it the catch-all room.....
It's clean and neat and you can use the bed
but filled with stuff I am waiting to go
throw and give away.**

*Always a muddle even if you try to organize
it. Mine has things in it that I don't know
what they are or what they are used for but
I dare not throw anything away!*

**Maybe this is a new chapter. A "catchall"
space, on a desk, on a table near the
outside door, etc., of "things" that are to
go somewhere, sometime...eventually! Our
family has had one for decades. I can't do
without it. And forget about my desk!
Junkpile.**

*I graciously "allowed" my husband one
kitchen drawer for his personal use. I
seldom open it...but when I do I shudder. I
sometimes...out of curiosity...paw my way
thru. Beyond the few small tools, flashlights,
and rubber bands, I see ATM receipts.
empty pill bottles, an old wallet, and there
are a few objects I don't even know what
they are! Once he starts having trouble*

getting that drawer to close he will spend an entire evening cleaning it out. I laugh of course and ask him why the heck he needs to stuff all that in there in the first place. Maybe some Psychologists would say we all do this mentally as well....stuff the issues we just can't deal with right now into some"drawer" in our brain...bring it out into the light of day when our heads too full! As good a system as any I guess for staying sane. I hope you all are staying safe during this crazy time!

You guys with drawers & rooms of junk are just beginners. I have the whole house !!

Well, my husband is officially a hoarder. All those eyeglass cases you get with your new glasses.? I just found a shoebox full of them in the garage. (he's a very neat hoarder.)

In 2012 my husband retired from highway construction supervisor. I found a stack of blueprints from completed projects 3 feet tall in our shop. I also found a stack of phone books just as tall.

There is an interesting selection of things in our medicine cabinet.

I have always had a junk drawer in which almost anything could be found. I think it's hereditary except my mom had many junk drawers. Mine is relatively small now.

Tidy the junk drawer and forget where anything is.

I got a new kitchen last year and moved the old set of cupboards into the shed so I could still keep my junk drawer as there isn't one in the new kitchen.

I think I have 3 what's in it junk drawers!

Also once I was so frustrated with it I just took a garbage bag and tossed it all dumped it ALL. Getting to that point again!

One time my ex said 'just throw it all out and start over'. LOL LOL

I have 3 junk drawers and a small cupboard.

I must confess I have multiple junk drawers!!

Beyond the Junk Drawer

There are many things we all seem to have in common or at least understand as we enter our senior years. Little habits, traits, and situations that travel beyond the confines of our little junk drawer. Here are just a few that were shared in our Junk Drawer discussion-

We walked to school and came home for lunch.

Living it up as Grandparents!! Getting to break all the rules we enforce on our children. Sugar them up and send them home.

Most of us have had the diseases for which they now have vaccines...chickenpox, mumps, measles. We were also the first ones to get polio shots. Most of us have photo albums, still cook, and vinyl record albums.

Being concerned about the hereafter, as in walking into a room and wondering what am i "hereafter."

Swearing up and down that every time I swat a fly, its carcass magically morphs into ten more of them to buzz into my life and give me something more to curse.

I'm at that wonderful age where the thing that filters what I say busted years ago and there are no replacement parts.

In life, there are two kinds of bullshit. One is a good fertilizer for your garden. The other is just bullshit.

I call things as I see them. Deal with it.

Going into another room and forget what you went in for.

Saving all found coins Because they are "pennies from heaven "

Wearing long-sleeved shirts even in the summer.

Recognizing the potential Velcro strapped shoes have to offer.....

Mix matched Tupperware - more lids than bowls or more bowls than lids!

Saving plastic bags.

Elastic waists on trousers.

Popping joints.

Keeping collections of items from our children's childhood...even when they tell us to get rid of it!

How about having a pair of reading glasses in every room?

Having home delivery of the newspaper.

(How many of these rang true to life for you? As you dive into reading the chapters within this book, I'm sure you will see we have many things in common in this stage of life. I hope that gives you comfort, reassurance, the ability to laugh at yourself and enjoy life a little more)

Out of the Mouths of Babes

Our Children and Grandchildren are the sources of our greatest moments of joy, and our funniest stories to share.

I asked our family of Sarcastic Seniors, to share their funniest wee one story, and here they are:

My grandson said – "It smells like a 'sit' house in here" (after someone had been in the bathroom for a while. He was 2.)

We had our youngest granddaughter in our car. She saw a bag of chips in the front of the car, and said "You allow food in your car? My daddy doesn't allow food in the car!" She looked at me with those big brown eyes and said, "I am a chip girl!" She was 2! She is now 37 with 3 kids of her own and yes they allow food in their car.

When my niece was young, it took a while to get her to knock on a closed door. One day, her dad was changing and she barged in. He immediately turned around, but not fast enough. He was in his underwear. Of course, being a kid, she asked, "What's

that?" "Oh, that's where I keep my socks."
Nothing more was said, and he asked her
to leave the room and shut the door. About
3 weeks later, she and her mom were
laying on the couch watch tv. She asked,
"Mommy, aren't you worried about
Daddy?" Her mom inquired why she should
be worried. My niece replied, "Well,
because of where he keeps his socks!" My
sister had no clue what she was talking
about. When she and my brother in law
compared notes, they couldn't stop
laughing!!!

While shopping in a large fruit and
vegetable shop my two boys approximately
3 and 6 were running around when I
overheard my eldest son telling the shop
assistant (but he's really hungry he's
starving) with a very serious face I may add.
OMG, I got out faster than Flash Gordon.

Turns out they were getting told off for
eating the grapes hanging over the counter.

This story didn't happen to me but my late
uncle. One Halloween the little boy that
lived down the street rang his doorbell. He

stood there in black boots, jeans, a yellow raincoat and a red fireman hat that had black socks attached to each side for ears, his face was painted white with black spots. My uncle opened the door and said: "Look at you, you're a dalmatian." The kid didn't skip a beat when he responded, "Nope, I'm a damn fire dog!" My uncle emptied his remaining candy into the kid's bag and turned off the light. That child had won Halloween!!

When my daughter had her last baby. I had made her enough lunches an suppers for a week. One was pork chops smothered in cabbage. My 9-year-old grandson said, Worst meal ever! Cracked me up.

I always ask my children on the drive home how their day was and what they learned in school. When my son was in K-5 the class had a unit on folk songs. He loved to sing and was so excited to share his new song with me but I was completely unprepared when he belted out at the top of his little lungs Jimmy CRAPPED corn and I don't care. Jimmy CRAPPED corn and I don't care...

My son said: "Mum, how can you have a boner if you don't even have a bone in your willy???"

Hmmm, didn't know WTH to say to that so simply responded with "Ask your father!!" lol. Couldn't stop laughing on the inside though! Where the hell does he come up with this stuff? More importantly, WHERE did he hear & learn about what a BONER is?

Once when I was a teenager we went to an Easter program at church & I has a friend's daughter on my lap. I was wearing a blouse with a pocket. The little girl, in the loudest voice she could muster grabbed my boob, which was under the pocket, & said What you got in your pocket? Naturally, everyone had to turn to see what was in my pocket.

My granddaughter looked very seriously at me during dinner one night and asked what a vegetarian was. She looked at me like I was crazy when I told her and promptly announced she was a 'Porkaterian'. Bacon for breakfast, ham for lunch, and ribs for dinner forever!

My car was at the garage getting some repair work done so my two-year-old son and I were on the bus. My son was extremely articulate at that age and was standing up on the seat chatting to two older women who were sitting behind us. He told them that we were going to see the doctor. One of the ladies asked him if he was sick. In a typically loud two-year-old voice he replied, I'm good but my mummy has a great big boil on her bum. Even the bus driver was laughing.

Well, my granddaughter at 5 yrs old told her friend that when God called her she was just going to tell him that she would stay at Mimi's.

Preschool days for our grandson he was reading a little book to his mom. "Alligators can grow to 24 feet & 2,000 pounds". He immediately looked up to his Mom & said: "That is bigger than Granny, right?"

A few years ago on my 52nd birthday, my granddaughter asked her mom, my daughter, "Mama how old is Boo"?

(that's what my kids call me). My daughter replied, "She is 52 years old today".

Little Missy's eyes got real big and she exclaims "Wow... she's almost 100"! Never felt so old in all my born days.

When my son patted my butt in a grocery store line and proudly announced to a complete stranger (with conviction!), "When I grow up I wanna have a big butt just like my mommy!" Yes, I wanted to die.

While picking up cake etc with my granddaughter Becky for her Mom's surprise party. I asked Becky, about age 3 1/2 if she would like to carry the balloons. Becky responded - "But Grandma, I will fly away"

Great-Grandma was giving 3-year-old great-grandson a cookie and she asked him, What's the magic word?

He enthusiastically replies, " Hocus Pocus!"

When my grandson was about 6 years old, his new stepfather was taking him to school. The discussion was height...his stepfather explained how even though his mom was short and petite, he might grow up to be big and tall like his grandpa because of his "genes". He asked my grandson if he understood what he meant... my grandson paused and said "yeah...I might be tall because my grandpa has pants.

My husband's name was Bob but everyone called him Bobby. So my son when he was 2 or 3 called him Bobby one day and we explained to him that he should not say Bobby but Daddy instead. One day he found a bobby pin on the floor brought it to me and said here Mommy, here's your daddy pin!

When my youngest daughter was about 3 and we were having Fried Chicken for dinner when I asked her if she wanted a leg ~ she thought for a minute and said 'no, I'll just have a hand!" LOL

Our neighbor's child was blessed with gorgeous red hair. One day at the grocery store a stranger approached them and said: "Hi there, Carrot Top!" The child

furrowed her brow and without missing a beat responded with "Potato Head!"

Once I was straightening my hair with a chemical straightener. My granddaughter was watching intently as I combed it smooth. She must have thought I was dying it, because she asked, "when you're done will your hair still be old?"

I had told her God lives in heaven, above the clouds so high you can't see him, later that day I was on a ladder with my head in the attic, and she asked me, hey Bonnie, do you see God up there? Lol

Running water to bathe my little son, I noticed the front of his shirt was filthy, but not one spot on the back. I asked him why, and he said "mommy, I wasn't working on that side". he always called being outside working!

When driving around the San Francisco beach area, I jokingly said oh that's the famous nude beach(not really). The young boys said yes let's go there...

I told them oh no, "when you've seen one, you've seen them all," the youngest said" but I haven't seen my first one yet"

My grandson said," I love bacon, I could marry bacon." " it would be a short honeymoon, though".

When my granddaughter was small, she used to crawl all over her grandpa. Once, while he was sitting in his chair, she happened to see the top of his head and said: "Papa, you have a hole in your hair!"

While traveling through Alabama, we stopped at a restaurant and our 4 y.o grandson asked if these people spoke Alabamaneese.

When my son was 4 or 5 years old, as we were leaving a store, standing on the other side waiting to come was a little person with a mustache and chin beard. My son turns to me and says loudly... MOM" THAT GUY SHRUNK.

My great-grandson,6 years old, requested this of me "make me something complicated for dinner!"

When my daughter was 4 we took a trip to CA. Our plane arrived at night and went straight to our hotel with our daughter asleep. She woke up looked around the room and disappointed and said: "This is California?"

When my youngest daughter was about 3, she calls bumble bee, bumbly bees.

On seeing the Christmas scene my granddaughter said oh look it the mommy and daddy and baby Genius.

Celso and a friend were having pizza for lunch. Celso told him "You should eat your crust because Jesus died on the crust"

Look, Grandpa, the baby looks just like you. She doesn't have a tooth in her head.

My daughter, almost 2, watching a water skier on the lake: Man chasing boat!!!

While trying to play a CD for my grandchildren I thought the batteries in the remote had given up Eldest said PA PA you have to have the TV switched on What a plonker I felt ???

My son at 5 "I want my mom and I know what she looks like " to my Aunt.

Look gramma, there's a fire fuck coming.

My son used to talk about hop grassers and flutterbies when he was about 4.

Speak to the finger cause you're not worthy of the hand.

(There really is so much love, laughter, and joy that comes from being around children.)

COVID-19

When the World Stayed Home

There are times in every generation that will go down in the history books and be remembered for decades to come. Pearl Harbor, 9/11, WWI, WW2, the Spanish Flu...

And, in 2020, we add to the list: COVID-19.

A virus originating in Wuhan China, it quickly took hold worldwide, and countries around the world found themselves shut in their homes for months to help slow the spread.

While writing this chapter, we are still dealing with COVID-19. Countries are slowing trying to open back up, people are trying to get back to work, and economies will be trying to make a comeback for years. And, there is no vaccine to date, so we expect this to rear its ugly head again this fall. We can only hope when it does, we are more prepared for the next round.

Cities looked like ghost towns. Businesses were closed, folks who could worked from home, and only essential businesses stayed open- Grocery stores, pharmacies, doctors' offices, essential factories, etc..

Many many people died, and the virus was hardest on the elderly or those with underlying health conditions. So, we had to isolate ourselves from our families to keep them and ourselves safe.

This has been a very trying time for all of us worldwide. And, knowing a pandemic will mostly like strike future generations as well, I turned to our wonderful Sarcastic Seniors and asked for their best bits of advice.

62 years young, Ashboro, NC.

Follow the old school advice of granny and grandpa. Stock a pantry for hard times, even if you don't see any, you rotate your foods in and out. Peanuts, cashews, walnuts sealed in cans and jars are good for a very long time and provide protein if the meat gets scarce, beef jerky is good to have on hand also. Keep an emergency 6 months worth of bill paying in the bank and a little nest egg of money at home in case you can't get to the bank or internet access. Stay calm, don't panic, and remember our ancestors survived far more deadly and trying times.

Always be prepared; Stay Calm and remember Good hygiene and common sense are "absolutely necessary " ... both of which at lacking in this generation!

Southern California

Be prepared - not just with food, but make sure you stock up on medications, pet food, etc. Overstock! the supply chain is coming back again, but prices are much higher than before. Listen to the health experts. Make sure you have things to do at home to keep healthy, happy, and sane. Keep in contact with others. Make sure that your home is in good repair. And plan to be in this situation much longer than first thought.

Toronto. Ontario, Canada.

Do your best to build up a year's salary in an emergency savings account. Do what the doctors and scientists say to do - NOT the politicians! Be prepared for the unexpected.

Stock up on household supplies, otc medications; prescriptions, and non-perishable food. Don't panic! Most importantly: make sure you're tuning into real news, not propaganda!

Be prepared, and make sure you get stuck with a person you really like. Keep a schedule, it helps pass the day if you tend to be bored easily. Read! The best to pass time is a quiet corner and a good book. All and all, it hasn't been too bad for me. I'm with someone I care about, I have my big kitty Bubba, got books, I'm a senior, don't run around much anyway, and I like staying home. Just a hassle with the masks and gloves and stuff. But is part of it. So do it, and keep safe.

Don't live in fear of the unknown. As others have said, we never know when our time on earth will be over and need to appreciate the small things along with the bigger events such as marriage, the birth of your children, the loss of a loved one. As a survivor of cancer, I went through the emotional loss of a part of myself and continued to have ups and downs for almost two years despite hearing "We got it all, everything looks good, etc." I kept waiting for the bad news to come. Finally came out the other side and decided I needed to start living my life and stop worrying about things I had no control over. With the virus and all the news, accurate or not, I decided I would stay informed, research as much as possible, protect not only myself but those I might be in contact with. Don't stick your head in the sand and say, "It can't happen to me, I'm too young, too healthy." A disease of any shape does not have a type, an age, a preference. Enjoy your lives each and every day, be kind to one another, find your peaceful spirit and if you have a belief system, lean on that. You don't have to go to church to believe in something bigger than yourself, because in the end, we are all part of a much bigger picture, but while we're here, be a good part of the bigger picture and make a positive impact each day. Ocala, FL

Listen to experts, scientists, not selfish politicians who are uninformed and spitting in the wind. I, according to my age,

am at risk. Look around at the ignorance of people who are protesting with guns. Is it fair to others not to follow guidelines because it's "inconvenient." Be responsible, respectful, and kind. Oh yes, load up on Tylenol, and toilet paper.

Epicenter, New Jersey

Wearing masks, eating chocolate, and enjoying my yard!

As Monty Python said, give a little whistle and always look on the bright side of life. Appreciate the little things in life. Be kind to each other. Smile and say hello to the person you pass on the street, you might just make them feel a little better. Love, not hatred and anger is the most powerful force on earth. From Peterborough, Ontario, Canada

Stay calm and don't panic. Listening to all the conspiracy theories will only make you anxious. Do protect yourself and your loved ones and care-care about yourself, your family, your pets, and everyone around you. Love goes a long way to helping you heal.-Nova Scotia, Canada

Stocking up on these things is why there was is a shortage. There was and is plenty of supply. Was the people's fear that caused the shortage.

From Catonsville Maryland.

Abide by the rules officials put in place. They have the big picture and more information than any individual. They have put the effort into trying to do the best thing for everyone. Take time to set up your household to always be prepared for an emergency situation, ie. keep a month of food and supplies on hand. Use your time wisely. we have time at home, I completed tasks I put off "till a rainy day." Take care of yourself. Eat healthily, take your vitamin supplements, exercise (ie. walking), communicate with friends and family. Give back to the community, if you can. Keep a positive attitude and don't forget to pray.

No matter where you are in life you need to have in stock supplies. Don't wait for an emergency to do that. Even an unexpected problem of any kind that interferes with employment makes a second disaster if no supplies are on hand. I did the blizzard of 78 and worked in a time when you may get your paycheck and layoff notice on the same Friday. No notice in the old days. I also watched the crazy stuff during the hurricane season in Florida when we lived there. Be prepared for the unexpected. I'm from Ohio.

Never take those you love, your job, your church, and your appreciation of going anywhere you want at any time for granted again.

Working again in Jasper, Alabama

From the mountains of Western Maryland...this part of history will go down as the worst medical/political coup in the USA. Pandemic created to fear and control people and how easily it was done. No doubt a bad virus, but found out not any worst than any other virus or disease...just poorly handled by big cities, thus, low numbers in rural America.

Make sure you don't run out of toilet rolls otherwise be none left in the shop the panic buyers amongst us will have bought them all Preston Lancs.

From Oregon. Starting with your first job save as much money as possible. When you buy your first home pay a bit more toward the principal.

Why not go into a vocation like a nurse, and you will have a job.

I think the first thing I would say is 'make sure you have in power a government who actually cares about the people not just about 'the economy', and aren't ignorant buffoons who ignore the scientists' advice as they prefer the thought of 'herd immunity'. Next, I would say is make sure, if you can, to have some savings so you don't starve to death, and lastly live somewhere where people are caring towards others and will help if necessary ie Scotland where I will be moving back to after this... Portsmouth, England

Pay attention to what happens with the government. If we had realized that over the past several (10+) years our government slowly disbanded the protocol and provisions for this type of emergency...would we have let it fly? Connecticut

Be calm, be sensible, remember the medical and food supply chains are very important, also remember that there is a lot more supporting the medical and food supply chains than just the health care workers, grocery stores, and transport. A lot won't be felt right away but if things don't start moving again the means of creating the protections and moving capability will start breaking down. And by all means, be aware of the people out there who will take advantage of others' misfortune any chance they get. North Carolina

Listen to the Doctors, NOT the politicians!!!

Be like Alaska...listen to your governor, follow the mandates and you be in phase 2 of reopening your state like us. We are all in this together.

From San Diego. Appreciate every day as none of us know how many we have.

Be careful who you elect!!

Northeast. Always vote. Live where you can be gainfully employed, your children can get a good education, and the local government demonstrates they have your best interest in mind.

Don't take anything or anyone for granted. Mt. Ida Arkansas

This too will pass. Delaware.

Quarantines are for those who are sick and at risk.

Western N C. Foothills, 68 years young, I remember the Polio epidemic, knew friends and relatives who bore the crippling results, being brought up out in the country, far from any heavily populated area, eight kids and a bootlegging father, who wasn't much help, an angel mother who never learned to drive, we never got to town hardly ever, never saw a doctor, going to school brought home measles, mumps, chickenpox, we survived those, finally received Polio vaccine when I was six years old, hopefully, a safe working

vaccine can be found for this too! Survival, whether its disease, hunger, poverty depends on the resilience of individuals, and the endurance to keep living.

It will never be in the history books as it played out. Our countries politicians are always, "if we can save one person" we will take the rights from everyone else. When we take that ONE person and heal them without everyone yelling it's racist, I want mine too, we will rewrite the history books.

That's why we have a constitution! Your freedom is a high price to pay for such an insignificant virus. Which was predicted to kill off hundreds of thousands! Never trust the government to watch what's best for you because you watch out for you and yours!

The stupid state of NY!

Protect yourself and others. Follow safety guidelines and use common sense! Life is precious, save it. Oh, and have a big savings account. From Taos, NM

The kids that are graduating from High School were born in 2001 the year of 9-11. You are right, this is a different chapter but we will be ok. Maybe we will not take so many things for granted!

The Sarcastic Seniors Alphabet

Imagine trying to learn the English Language, if you were taught by seniors, who only referenced words as they related to our senior lives.

That was the challenge posed to our delightful group, and once again, they surpassed my expectations.

Here is your Alphabet for Seniors:

A is for:

Arthritis and Aloe

B is for:

Bunions, Bowel Movement, Booze, Ben-Gay, and Benzedrine

C is for:

Colonoscopy, Cane, Compression Socks, Cataracts, Calamine, Corns, and CRS (Can't Remember Shit)

D is for:

Dentures, Depends, and Discreet Liners

E is for:

Eyeglasses, Eating Out, Early Bird Special, ECG, Erectile Dysfunction, and Elastic stocking

F is for:

Funerals, Forgetfulness, Family, and Fiber

G is for:

Grandchildren, Geritol, Groans, and Gout

H is for:

Hair Loss, Hearing Aids, Heating Pads, Hot Flashes, Huh? and High Blood Pressure

I is for:

Itchy Skin, Insomnia, Invalid, and Indigestion

J is for:

Juice Cleanse, Joint Pain, and Joy

K is for:

Knowledgeable, Kinks, Knee Replacement, and Kindness

L is for:

Lanai, Loss of Memory, Love, and License

M is for:

Motivation, Memory Loss, Muscle Aches, Medicare, Mobility, Memories, Miralax, and Menopause

N is for:

News Channel, Nursing Home, Naps, Neuropathy, Nostalgic, and Night Sweats

O is for:

Opinionated, Optimism, Osteoporosis, Old, and Osteoarthritis

P is for:

Pills, Prostate Exam, Prune Juice, Prescriptions, and Pill Case

Q is for:

Quilts, Questions, and Quiet

R is for:

Retirement, Recliner, Rolaids, and Relaxed

S is for:

Sarcastic Seniors, and Senior Discounts

T is for:

Teeth in a Cup, and Tremors

U is for:

Urologist

V is for:

Viagra, Vitamins, and Vertigo

W is for:

Wrinkles, Wisdom, Weight Gain, Walking Stick, White Hair, Wise, and What did you say?

X is for:

X-Rays

Y is for:

Yawns, and Young at Heart

And...

Z is for:

Zantac and ZZZs

Special Thanks to all of our wonderful Sarcastic Seniors for this funny and true list.

And, thank you, for being able to laugh through the Aging Process.

A sense of humor is so important, and so abundant within this wonderful group.

Stretching the Retirement Income

Brian and I are now approximately 2 years from retirement. Wondering if we will have enough to not only survive but thrive and enjoy those Golden Years together, is a constant on our minds.

We don't live a fancy life. We take one vacation a year, rarely eat out, and our one big occasional splurge is going to a good music concert.

We have narrowed down our retirement place to the Oregon Coast. It has weather that is much kinder than the Brutal Iowa summer heat and nasty winters. However, the cost of living is higher on the coast than here in the Midwest.

Rent is very high there, so we have decided on a manufactured home. And, we will probably both have part-time jobs to enable us to still travel and enjoy life while our health enables us.

But, it is still going to take some conscientious budgeting and planning, to be able to afford the life we envision.

So, of course, I asked our favorites, the Sarcastic Seniors, for their money-saving tips to STRETTCCCCHHH those retirement bucks. Here is what they had to say:

Offer the hooker half the asking price.....

One has to pay off debt. Then ask one's self before shopping, "Do I really need this or do I just want it?" Have a savings account, even if the deposit is small. Check out free forms of entertainment. Get to know your local library. If you live alone, that doesn't mean that you have to be lonely. Do something nice for someone. Go to church.

My bucks won't stretch. The few I have are brittle and even the self check out at the food stores keep spitting them back out...But for real, the only one I can suggest is to stop buying coffee out. But before you do...you know, "borrow" a few of those self-service take out cups & lids then make your own before you go.

I'm planning to retire in another 8 years and have started to pay off debt and spend less. I shop at dollar stores for everyday items.

Pay off credit cards even if only a few dollars over the minimum each month.

I turn off Central unit @ least every other late evening until morning. I have a small fan in the living room & ceiling fans are always on. Have energy efficient bulbs in overhead lights. Night light in bathroom & hallway. Water is always minimal. Never use hot water for laundry, add 1/4 to 1/2 cup of Vinegar to full load. Hang out sheets, pillowcases, socks & underwear - Made a cloths line between corner posts off Deck! Clothes always smell great. Never use softeners anymore. The vinegar softens clothes & they smell fresh always.

We sold a rental and bought an older, low mileage motorhome and a campground membership. We travel the US and Canada full time. For our dues of $800/year, we have over 160 campgrounds to choose from. We love our traveling life. No matter where we are, campground, parking lots,

the middle of the desert, or along the ALCAN, we are always home. Less expensive than house/yard maintenance and much more fun.

I changed all light bulbs to led ones. Free offers, on sale, etc. It did help my electrical bill. But the company keeps hiking the rate. All gains lost. Still not a bad thing to do. Buy on sale. We also "turn the heat down " at night. And wear a sweater in the day. Take advantage of senior discounts at a lot of stores. Don't be afraid to ask if they have it. It all adds up to a bit of savings. Make your coffee at home. Go easy on take-out food. There is a lot to give up but it does add up and you don't really miss it. Yah do I really need a new shirt !!!????

We seldom eat out. And make sure you have a good vehicle and no payments before you retire. You may never be able to afford a new vehicle after retirement.

Set aside 10% of income per month for yourself. Kinda like a bank at home.

I will be debt-free when I retire in 83 weeks (584 days) and have the house completely redone - enjoy it for a year, then move. Pulled in the belt so I'll be used to living on a pittance.

As soon as I retired I called the electric and gas companies and enrolled in their monthly budget plans. That way we knew what our bills would be each month. I also pay them directly out of a bank account each month so I'm never late.

Well, it might be too late for some, but a 401k invested in secure stock helped me. 45 years working in factories with the 401k in the last thirty, bought us a fairly new house, he inherited property, retired in the country, no mortgage, just medical, utilities, food, life insurance to pay, no expensive trips, just putter around the house, garden, stay away from yard sales, flea markets, we've got all the clothes, shoes, Whatnots, and dodads we will ever need, a few health problems to maintain, otherwise life's good.

I have all the apps that apply to bills I have such as Dish, insurance, etc. I can go to the apps and see exactly what I'm paying for. Just last week I was able to adjust my preferences on 2 apps saving $50 per month.

Make sure you read the flyers of your favorite grocery store, Buy a little more if on sale Plan your menus accordingly.

Food pantries, soup kitchens, and discounted fares on the buses. No takeout food.

Stay away from online shopping and home shopping channels! Too easy to spend money. Money not spent is money saved!

Debt-free, only buy what I can afford, live simply, and single!

One way I save that hasn't been mentioned here is using the library for books, movies, and magazines. Also, when you prepare food make enough for a couple of meals. The major cooking is done once, the extras are frozen and/or reheated. Family-sized meats are generally cheaper.

I make a menu out for a month, make my grocery list off if it and try not to go back all month. I bought yeast so I can make bread if. I run out and powdered milk for cooking with. I would guess I spend a little more than 1/2 of what I used to spend.

Be sure to set up a budget and try to stick to it!

I stay at home most of the time. Work in the yard, quilt, watch movies, and now that summer is here, swimming in the back yard and BBQ.

Only buy needs not wants.

A new hairstyle that doesn't cost over $500 a year.

The Significant's Insignificants

We love our significant others. We can't imagine life without them. Then, why is it, that the littlest things turn into our biggest pet peeves about them, and send our skin crawling every time we witness?

My husband Brian, is a GEM. Plain and Simple. I am blessed beyond belief to have found love later in life with this wonderful man. That being said, some little things drive me crazy!

The biggest one we shall name "Chippiness". I am a very happy person, except in the morning. It takes a good hour and a half, to hit the nice switch, and until that happens, I just want to quietly reside in Bitchville, USA.

Said husband of mine, wakes up each day, like a little kid on Christmas morning, just beaming with happiness. It irks me to no end.

And, I am sure that there are plenty of things that send him through the roof about me. Number 1 on the list, would be the

"Honey-do" lists I am constantly making. I have found in the past couple of years that my memory is not as good as it used to be, and the only way I complete all of the things I need to is by writing them down. But, I have also in the process inflicted my lists onto Brian. Let me tell you, he is NOT a fan of the yellow sticky notes.

I threw this subject out to our beloved Seniors and asked them to share the things their significant other does that drives them crazy. There are some doozies. Enjoy!

I live alone and love it!

Never, I mean never, closing anything he opens. Drawers, cabinets, toolbox, anything that opened. I would just close them, wasn't worth my energy to fight...

My hubby as been gone for a few years now but if I had to pick one thing it would be him waiting till the last minute to get ready to go somewhere. If I have to be late I would rather not go at all.

I can't catalogue all my faults but they are legion. I am messy, unorganized, and do not always hear directions clearly. Three issues that could lead to divorce. I think my husband's placidness in a heated moment bugs me most. But truth be told there has to be a ying to my yang. Forty years married in July and this is a little thing, easy to ignore.

When you get older like we are. 80. Lots of things don't work the way they used to. In our case, we are both hard of hearing and both have hearing aids that cost thousands of dollars. I'm happy to wear mine so I can hear better. My wife of 58 years doesn't like to wear hers because, among other things, she is "not good with technology." Consequently, I have to shout and repeat everything. Now, this isn't humorous, and this isn't a little thing. So, seriously, I've stopped talking to her when she isn't wearing her aids. We can't have good conversations and many of the great pleasures of communicating like jokes, observations, small talk, are lost.

We've attended hard of hearing support groups where this has been discussed so I know she has heard this "complaint" from others as well as from me. I know this isn't

in the spirit of the humor of sarcasm in senior relationships. I can deal with all the funny things, but this issue is one that I just can't fix or get passed. I find myself making sarcastic remarks but they are never heard...and perhaps that a good thing.

I'm the wake-up and smile... the other half is a zombie for several hours so I guess I am the irritating one.

Botany is his passion, all he ever talks about, speaks to me in Latin a lot. I read a lot, and he is nattering on and on about how many species of pines or firs or whatever there are in our area (they are all Christmas trees to me). I am glad he has a passion, but he has a few talks about botany and repeats them over and over and over again. He will quiz me about plants to see if I remember. I keep telling him to read a book so he can come up with new conversations!

He'll ask me what I want (for dinner, TV show I want to view) and then proceeds to tell me what he thinks I really want after I've answered him.

My husband has to come into my bedroom and explain in detail what he's watching on TV, while I'm trying to watch something else!

Not married but have a live-in. The same thing opens a cabinet it stays open. Open a package, leave the debris laying even those little things on a loaf of bread. Chip bags closed up tightly but left wherever he's eating them. I just ask "are you done here?" Then put it away, dispose of it, or close the cabinets.

His inability to put things back in the cupboard.

My husband trimmed his mustache and nose hairs over the sink and NEVER cleaned the sink out.

He doesn't put things away after using them. I don't say anything. Bless his heart.

Going into a room, turning on the light, and then leaves the room, light still on. Every. Darn. Time. Married 52 years.

My husband did crossword puzzles and when he thought would click the ballpoint pen. Drove me crazy (daily) now that he's gone I miss hearing that click.

My husband being RETIRED and home 24/7. My workload has quadrupled since he's now home!!!!

My Wife simply will not put her Wet Towels in the Laundry Basket Ever! Married 34 years

Turning on a light or radio in a room I'm occupying and then leaving the room.

Offering or promising to do something, never getting around to it, then accusing me of nagging if I ask him about it.

Hearing my husband mispronounce Robert Mitchum as 'Meechum'.

Incapable of refilling the soft soap dispenser, replacing the empty paper towel roll, and getting the clothes INTO the laundry basket/hamper, instead of the floor right next to the hamper.

To name a few..............

Hubby likes to build things, which is awesome. While I support his hobby, I don't need to hear every step of that building process, what kinds of screws, nails, boards, tools...the list is endless, along with how each one is used. Plus, he's dumbing it down for me, ie, 'mansplaining'.

I've thought about this. In years past I probably could have come up with as they say some real doozies. But now after 52 years, I can't think of a thing. I'm just really glad we're still together and have some good conversations. Some not. But we still laugh at the same stuff.

I have not had a significant other for many years. Many many years. But I often find myself confronted by other women's husbands in stores offer expert advice, including taking an item out of my basket and replacing it with one they prefer!

Breathing...just plain breathing.

Picks his fingers.

My late husband, every time we passed a sign saying "Garage Sale" he would say--

Hey, someone's selling their garage. It was funny the first 5 or 6 times.

Eats too loud, and wakes up every morning lol.

Whistling when he is working is the first thing that comes to mind.

I think Brian should get up his normal, chipper self and start making lists of things for you to do.

Never I mean never closing a drawer and sometimes doors!

I am an organized hoarder, my big fault. My husband is not so when he doesn't like where I put something, he will put it up where it is never to be seen again and he forgets where it is. Also, after 30 years in the same house, he has yet to find the dishwasher which is beside the sink. He just puts dishes and utensils in the sink. I do love him.

My husband rubs his feet together when he's going to sleep. It makes me want to hold a pillow over his face until he stops.

Not putting garbage in the can. Just leaving it on the sink!!!

My husband takes his socks off, and leaves them either inside out, in a ball, or a weird combo of both. I. Hate. Feet!!! Having to touch those stinky socks just f*cks me up!!!

TV remote choosing a film of his choice and then falling asleep, lowering the volume halfway through a film because suddenly it's too loud or changing the program because he's bored without asking.

Tuning me out.

Watching tv. He falls asleep and snoring. I turn the channel and he says why did you change that. I was watching it.

Caressing his stick shift (in the car) with his thumb.

WARNING: Do not answer that question...You will pay!

Breathing! All the bloody time....in out in out...on and on and on...drove me mental! Divorced now.

(It was that or a long spell in prison!)

It's Inevitable

It's a law of nature, and there is no way to avoid the "Theory of Inevitability". As we get older, it is just another one of those things that we grudgingly accept, and sometimes even laugh about.

I can spend 2 hrs getting ready, and have perfect hair and makeup on for a date day out, and we will not run into a single person.

But, should I need one quick thing from my local drug store, and go in with sweats and no makeup, it is a freaking class reunion.

And, it is not just me, here are some tested situations for the Theory of Inevitability, as shared by our Sarcastic Seniors.

It's inevitable that if I use up all the cream for my coffee, I won't remember I needed to go to the store until I am tucked in bed that night!

It's inevitable---if I water the garden and lawn, it will rain.

Mow my yard and it rains and grows faster!

I get a stimulus check and I then need a tree taken down because the last storm had it leaning way too far for comfort...and, of course, it will be more than the stimulus check.

If it's 3:00 am, I have to pee.

It's inevitable--when I bathe the dog, it will go out & roll in the dirt!

It's inevitable if I start a diet I'm invited to a birthday party.

If I take a nap, I'll need to get to the bathroom.

When I get a nice lazy day to relax and do nothing family members call needing me to do something or go somewhere.

It is inevitable - an unexpected windfall check arrives in the mail, appliances vie for which will irreparably break down and you HAVE to buy a new one! I swear they know when you open the envelope!

If I clean the litter box...my cats going right in...

It's inevitable if I mop the floor the dog will throw up on it.

When I lay down to take a nap the cat decides it's time to play.

It's inevitable if there is music in the store I will dance pushing my cart.

If a squadron of Geese in V formation fly over my parked car...

If I like a TV show it gets canceled after one season.

Nothing lasts forever: Youth, wrinkle-free skin, or life.

It's inevitable if I'm downstairs my phone will ring upstairs.

Life, in three words...It's Inevitable..."It Goes On".

That time will sneak up on me!

It's inevitable- if my bank balance is zero, there will be a sale of a lifetime going on!

As soon as I sit down in the bathroom ... that phone rings downstairs.

If I wash my windows it will rain.

Make some lunch... someone stops for a visit.

If I enjoy taco Tuesday...

Wet fart Wednesday always follows.

It's inevitable...if a man likes me...he's either a pervert or....nah...just a pervert.

If I make a comment, someone else has already said that.

It's inevitable that when I post anything on FB I get censored...

I'm sure it was inevitable that you saw yourself in many of these as well.

Are you Lonely Alone?

For those of you who are living alone, by circumstance or by choice, do you wish to someday share life with someone?

Brian and I were friends and worked together for many years, and after my late husband died of cancer, this friendship eventually turned into love, and then the marriage I am so happily living.

But whether folks are single again through a divorce or being widowed, I wondered how many were hoping for love again someday, or how many were embracing the single life.

So, I asked the experts, my beloved Sarcastic Seniors.

A little over a year ago my husband was diagnosed with cancer. It came out of the blue for us and it has been a hard year. He is doing well and has been given 10 to 15 years. He is 75. We live in a rural area and he had to go away for treatments so I was home alone. It gave me a taste of what life would be like on my own. I would never want anyone else but him. It was a sad and lonely time for both of us. We are extremely close. I could and would do it but I don't want to. Were celebrating 50 years in December.

It would be nice to meet someone to share time with; maybe go places together and who knows ... it just might become more, but if it just remained friendship, that's fine too.

I've been alone now for 9 years and I'm beginning to think it's just not going to happen.

I'm a widow as of 2 years ago, I didn't think I could live alone, but I found I enjoyed my freedom. I seemed to be content with friends, but after a while, I found that I was missing out on the intimacy between a man and a woman. I have been dating a man for about 5 months now. It's been good so far, but I doubt I will ever want marriage again. I want both worlds, freedom and space along with companionship, but who

knows. That might change, but I won't hold my breath.

I don't know. I tried sharing a house with someone. Didn't work out. He wanted to control and I have an aversion to being controlled. I am an introvert so I like my alone time but I do miss not having someone to share my day with, to talk with, etc.

Very lonely living alone after the loss of a loved one! Miss my late husband beyond words.

The same thing happened to me. My husband died and a friend I knew for 30 years at work stepped up to help me. A year later we were married and have had the happiest 20 years of our lives!

I'm 64 and I've been alone for the past six years. I can't say what will happen in the future, but I like my freedom. I was married to a very controlling man, and I've been divorced for 20 years. I've had one semi-serious relationship since then, but he told me it was him or the cat. I didn't choose him.

I honestly don't know. It's been 6 years since my husband died. We were together for 38 years and had a very good & successful marriage, So, I have a very high standard. I've decided I don't want "seconds"---if I have anything it will have to be an encore. And you don't hunt for encores----part of what makes them special is that they are unexpected.

I was married at 23. I wouldn't recommend it. I married a man 13 years older than me. He passed away when I was 34. I was a single parent for seven years. I remarried at 40. I had another child at 41. We were divorced 12 years later.

I was on my own again and frankly loved it. My eldest was gone and my baby was 12. Things were good. Money was tight. Then, I met someone who I thought was the one I had waited for! We have been together for 7 1/2 years. Married for a year. While he has good qualities I think I should have stayed single. I feel from the era I was raised one felt you had to be with someone. I have made poor choices. The

two things that bring me joy now are my dogs!

I became a widow 4 years ago. It took a while to adapt. The sad saga of me is that I would always be comparing anyone new to my husband. He was my best friend and partner in all ways. I will just remain single and enjoy my friends.

I completely enjoy the peace and quiet of living alone after working hard all my life and constantly having family members living with me for one reason or another.

Yes, at times I would like some male companionship but prefer not marriage. After 9 years of being a widow, I enjoy answering to no one about where I am going and how much I am spending.

My husband recently passed away. Even tho he was easy to live with I prefer to be alone. What I miss is having someone to talk too, I don't need to be married for that.

I've lived alone for a long, long time... I've always wished I could find someone special *to share the remainder of my life with... but I have a deep-down feeling I won't ... which I guess is ok ... I'm glad I'm a strong woman who holds their own.*

1976 was my freedom year. With three daughters to raise and a couple of career changes I find that although I have "opportunities " I cannot become "a nurse with a purse."

I was married for 53 years. I followed him around the world.

We had 2 children, 3 grandchildren, and one great-grandchild.

Now I eat what I want to eat when I want to eat.

Yes, I'd like a companion to go places with.

But I won't marry again. Lots of reasons to not get married at my age.

Alone does not equal lonely. I am my own best company.

I met my now husband 4 years after my first husband of 39 years died of cancer..we have been married for 9 years...we give each other space and are there for each other when needed. He accepts me for who I am and I accept him for who he is. No regrets.

I'm ok by myself widowed almost 18 years ago, stayed alone for almost 3 years. I was in a bad relationship for 10 years (I thought I could keep him sober) NOT! I've been alone for 5 years and it's better than being with somebody who doesn't appreciate you. So, I'm fine alone.

The saddest thing for me is having so much to tell and no one to tell it to.

I think for myself not getting married until I was 43 helps a lot. I had lived alone from 17 to 41 so being married was a huge challenge. But it made me strong and confident to be solo again.

I chose the road less traveled for a woman...I lived in a small rural area and Didn't want to get married and have children. I wanted to see the world and was so fortunate and blessed to have parents that allowed me to do that without the guilt trip! I have been all over this country and part of Europe. I always knew I would return home if my parents got sick. They did, I came home, and took care of them and one of my Dad's brothers who had no children. Longer story short, I am now in the house, on the farm where I grew up. Both parents and Uncle are gone but I am very content to be here and alone. But have never been lonely. I love my life. Not sure I could get used to being with somebody all the time, but if it happens, that's ok. If not, that's ok too! I love your posts!

I think I would be ok living alone as long as I was living near others. A condo situation would be ideal. I like my alone time and tend to be somewhat particular, so I think I'd be best on my own, but spending time here and there with someone who felt similarly.

After 2 failed marriages & 8 years single a man entered my life. I asked him to marry me. It's been 20 years now. I never knew I would never have to work another day in my life. Keep your heart's open and receptive to what you may not even see or hear but... just feels right.

I have been alone off and on my whole life. It's not what I had in my head. But I have such a terrible track record with men. I do not trust my judgment. Yes it gets lonely, yes I wish I had someone in my life but I am stuck in my fear. On the upside, I make my own decisions, no one to try to run my life, thoughts, and feelings. What I would like is friendship with a man, not a ruler.

I miss having a partner to study the Bible with and go places with. He was Navy and I served in the Army, so we had lots of fun battles. I miss just sitting and listening to him talk about his military days. I miss walking with him, and of course the cuddle and romantic times. People were created to be in couples.

I truly believe the deepest, sincere relationships, start as friendship...

I am 63 and twice divorced. My second husband left me for his grade school crush after 20 years of marriage and two kids. I own my part in the breakup but how he did it has devastated me emotionally and it still hurts deeply after 6 years. As a result, I have *major trust issues. I like being single and not having to answer to anyone but myself!*

I like living alone. Been married 3 times, been on my own for the last 15. I have grandkids and a dog! Life is good! I keep busy.

No. Don't want anyone. I am far too content in my own company.Independent.Love my solitude. Not lonely. I am 68.

On my own now for 35 years. I just turned 71 but will always feel like a kid inside lol. Raised my 5 kids and didn't date while doing that and then it was past my time I guess. I do feel lonely but love life and guess these are the cards I was dealt.

Funny how times have changed. Years ago all young women wanted was marriage. now it seems women don't but men do. I wonder why that is? It could be that back in the day women weren't independent and depended on men to take care of them. I have taken care of a husband and kids for so long, that I like just taking care of me.

Alone and would not mind a partner with his own income like me but only one who never tells me what to do. I manage just fine on my own otherwise.

I live on my own and I'm content to remain that way. I don't want to bring any problems by having my life/kids/grandkids critiqued by an outsider. I'm set in my ways.

I would have a hard time having someone underfoot all the time. I can do what I want to do when I want. Part-time is ok.

Divorced over 27 years now and completely single for over 9 years. I would NOT have it any other way!

I don't want to be on my own but I had met a violent partner years ago then met unsuitable men after him so I am on my own for now.

Don't know where to start....she can swim.

Been a widow for almost 7 years and would love to find a good significant other.

No, I prefer to remain alone, but it probably won't be too long before I'm no longer able to be alone. I am 68.

I wouldn't trust anyone again 42 yrs marriage down the pan to a serial cheater. I could write a book!

Nah... I'm content alone. More peaceful.

Alone for 30 years. Content.

Nope. No. No way!

My husband and I met at 63 and 59, respectively. He was widowed, I was divorced. In our 5 years together, we have had MORE fun than a bag of hammers. We greet every day knowing it could be our very last day of happiness before the inevitable strikes. We are joyful. So are you. That matters.

I became single 9 years ago. It was very difficult at first, but I found I like doing what I want when I want. But yes, I do miss hugs and kisses and companionship. My job and lifestyle don't afford opportunities to meet men. Unless I was to stand on a street corner and advertise! Maybe someday...

The Guilty Pleasures

Things change as we age. There is no denying or changing that fact. It hit me yesterday while I was waiting for a knock on the door.

I was waiting for my grocery delivery. It is now one of the things I love most. I will cut corners wherever necessary to make sure that is something I can continue to afford.

When I was younger, my guilty pleasures were gold charms from every stop in my travels, trips to the Caribbean, and lingerie.

Now that I am older, less is more in the jewelry department, the heat drives me insane, and please- lingerie is an oversized t-shirt and jammie pants.

But, I ADORE grocery shopping from the couch without a stitch of makeup on, not dealing with the weather, and no one hitting me in the ankles with their cart.

The grocery delivery guy is one of my favorite people in the world.

I posed this topic out to our favorite seniors, and you know they had lots to say.

Books. Real paper books. No Kindles or e-readers. And I like to keep a couple waiting while I finish the three I'm currently reading; one in the bedroom, one in the living room, and one in my car.

Mine used to be jewelry now I could not survive without my grocery deliveries.

Mine is the same as yours and darned proud of it.

Reading whenever the mood strikes. Fan of real books!

Fish n Chips!!!!

Lays Honey BarBQ Chips... now I'm hungry

Oh, and Jigsaw puzzles.

Amazon I even get surprised sometimes on Mondays from shopping on Friday or Saturday nights.

I shop alone...currently every 3rd week on seniors day/time...but alone. Hubby impulse buys but also thinks its the Indy

500 - in and out in minutes. I like to look, I have my list and I stick to it but I do like to see what's new. I can give him a list but he always comes home with tons of snacks. Now I tell him I need to check out the birthday cards or something else that he would find equally boring so he opts to stay home. It isn't that I don't want him along but at the moment we are together waaaay too much.

My manicure, pedicure, and yes, the waxing off of the hair on my face!!

I love my Audiobooks, I can listen to them and do jobs around the house at the same time.

If you feel guilty or let anyone else make you feel guilty for something you enjoy... Do not accept a laid on guilt trip... it is a method of control by one who is jealous.

Sometimes I feel a little guilty about doing nothing but it soon passes!

Grocery shopping from my favorite chair, on my tablet. It's exciting for me as I don't have to go to the grocery store and wait in line anymore!

Grubhub for dinner. We've eaten food from places that I've never been to!

Debunking fake news on FB by providing the real facts that have been fact-checked. (I'm a retired teacher who loves to research, I know I'm odd)

Sipping my coffee slowly while lounging in my house dress, no hurry, I'm retired now!

Online shopping although I do try to use local shops when I can. A girl has gotta have yarn.

Frozen caramel mocha latte. Going out to dinner, getting massages and my hair done..hopefully, I can do them again.

Mine seems to be lingering over morning coffee. Blessed to be retired so I can do that every day. LOL

My Lindt 78 percent cocoa bars. A few squares in the evening and I'm good.

Hate to say it, but ice cream. This is something new for me I think it's caused by COVID. Luv!

Traveling which I no longer can do.

My weekly trip to the salon to get my hair done.

Coffee with a splash of Carmel whiskey, a quiet morning on my deck, and no one talking to me while I enjoy it.

Crafts. Mostly papercrafts. It's what keeps me sane.

Clothes shopping and shoes. Now it's strictly food.

I have become addicted to my baths with bath bombs.

The wings combo from the place around the corner. Once a week. #quarantinebody #sorrynotsorry

Sitting around a table having a meal and laughing with my BFFs.

Britbox, Acorn, and Amazon and hot ginger tea.

A ciggie, a coffee while watching the sunrise.

Same, no carrying stuff up the steps!

Mani-pedi.. don't do it often

Watching kDrama whenever I can.

Friends Family snacks films and TV

The sound of water flowing thru rocks

Don't know anymore... have to think about it...

love to travel

Staying up late and sleeping in

Crisp's tv and family

my comfy couch.

Ordering dinner.

Pedicures.

Books.

True crime!

Shoes

omg yes, everything delivery...

Jelly beans. Jelly Belly.

Menudo. Prune cake.

Reality tv.

Ice cream and brownies

Hookers and blow. Every other month, know your limit.

Pineapple empanadas.

Christmas in July

2020 has been a crazy year. Covid-19, riots, sky-rocketing unemployment, and a failing economy have left most of us just wanting to move on to 2021, and leave this year in the dust.

After 6 months of being home, and watching the news every day, I decided to move this year along, and start celebrating the Holiday season. So, this morning, on the 4th of July weekend, I put up the Christmas tree. Yes, you read that right.

I think we are at the age where we can do what we want. I don't have to "like it or lump it". And, I am just exhausted with the state of our world.

So, you know between the 4th of July, and Christmas also comes Thanksgiving. And, I gave that some pause as well.

One thing this shut-in has taught me- I am thankful. For the blessings in my life. Our wonderful family, those friends that are unwavering and filled with true love, and most of all for my Husband.

I think any man that has to look at his wife working from home with no makeup and Jammie pants on for 6 months in a row, without complaint is a true blessing. And, more than that, he tells me daily, that this hot mess I have come to be is beautiful.

He needs glasses desperately, but is not getting them. I love him just the way he is.

We are getting close to the big R-retirement, and I have been wondering if we wouldn't kill each other spending all day together. But this shut-in time has shown me, we will be fine, and will keep a sense of humor above all.

I guess the thing I really wanted to say by putting up the Christmas tree, is that, no matter what is going on in the world around us, keep some celebration in your life. If you need too, skip the news now and then, go for a walk and just enjoy nature, unplug from social media for a couple of days, take a drive- whatever you have to do to smile.

So, once the tree was up, I also couldn't resist rewriting a Christmas song, for Brian to sing for our Sarcastic Seniors.

This is sung to the tune of 'White Christmas'. Here are the lyrics:

I'm Dreaming of 2021

I'm Dreaming of 2021,

When all this COVID crap is gone.

When we can go out Shopping,

And even bar hopping,

And, all People get along.

I'm Dreaming of 2021,

With front row concert seats again.

There are Football and Baseball,

In March There'll be B-Ball, and

Things are normal once again.

Always find ways to Celebrate life, my friends.

The Rebellious 'Seenager'

As Seniors, we have reached the point in our lives, where we don't have to answer to others, and we can make decisions, based on what we want and need for ourselves. We no longer have to conform to any 'norm'.

I don't care if everyone is wearing the latest style, if it isn't comfortable, I am not wearing it.

If I don't want to do something, I have learned to politely decline. No excuses, I just don't want to.

I don't care if everyone else is getting tucks, nips, and going to the salon every week. Last year I got tired of the never-ending dye job, and trying to ward off the greys, and said "Welcome". I am now waiting for my new silver hippie to fully emerge.

Our Wonderful Sarcastic Seniors also offered up the following as proof, that I am not the only Rebellious Seenager. Enjoy!

Love hearing my teen grandkids explaining that playing scrabble-type games and bingo on my phone makes me a "gamer" too.

Haven't been to the salon since Feb. I have about 3" of salt & pepper roots showing and I like it! Have an appointment Monday, think I'll stop coloring too! She is closing her salon anyway!

I learned to say no a long time ago. Now I say "because I don't want to"

I'll have to whisper this. I don't want to cause a fuss... Freed my girls right after I retired.

We kept those girls corralled for years, it is time to let them roam free!

I speak up when someone is rude (breaks in line), etc. One day a woman asked me if I might be afraid after the incident as the man was yelling at me. I said no. That I had lived a good life and was tired of putting up with rudeness. She said she wished she could be that brave. And I used to be shy.

I have discovered ponytail baseball caps. No more curlers or flat irons or trying to cover the spots where the hair is thinning. I do believe these wonderful little items will become part of my standard wardrobe. I just hope I can find some with lace or sequins for those occasional dress-up affairs I'm forced to attend.

For me its about comfort. So my sneakers are not the most current. Who cares? My jeans are comfy, not fashionable. My hair might not be quite up to whatever standards are considered the norm...again...who cares? It's white, its usually pretty short (A la Judi Dench style) but currently with no haircuts, it has become a wavy Doris Day and no I will not sing...I like my family and friends and wouldn't inflict that upon them.

I spit out my food onto the floor when I don't like it and I tell the cook to get another job. I say "no" when I don't want to do something. And, I head-butted my minister.

Gran, as I took up playing hefty video games after he said he had a game I might like...sure did.

I've always done what I wanted (more or less). Now that I'm old, when people get more patronizing with me, I never give them the benefit of the doubt, I give them the full range of my sarcasm with a raised voice.

I am 65 and fight for my individuality everywhere I go.

Just like saying what I am feeling. If it shocks too bad... I have been good All my 60 plus years. So excuse me I am making up for lost time.

I enjoy letting an a$$h@le know they're an a$$h@le... Just might help one take a look at themselves and make a complete turnaround...Na, probably not !!!

I always resented the time at the hairdressers having my hair colored. So when I retired it was the first thing to go. I never regretted it.

I like being able to say NO with a smile.

I'm 78, have natural color, long hair, wear overalls, and walk about 5 miles a day!

Aging- The Numbers Game

The older we get, the more apt we are to use little tricks and numbers to muddle through our daily lives. It's a part of aging, and if we can keep a sense of humor with it, our days are more interesting.

For me, my favorite number to remember is 1. That is the number of times we get to enjoy this thing called life. Remembering that when little things go wrong helps keep me grounded and focused on the prize of a life well-lived.

My least favorite number of late is 4. That appears to be the number of times I have to enter, exit, and re-enter a room before I can remember what I went in there for in the first place.

When I tossed this out to our resident experts, here is what a few of them had to say:

5- # of times Checking my pockets, for my Keys, Wallet, Phone, .. oh also my Meds, hanky, warm jacket, or a hat. Oh, stuff it, ill just watch tv and have a nap.....

3- the number of times I have to check to make sure I put the right meds in the right place in my pillbox.

1000- If I told you once I've told you a thousand times!

3 - when you are talking with your friend and telling a story and get all going with another story and end up forgetting what you were talking about, LOL

2- Heard this on my way home today: you die twice. First, when life leaves your body. Second, the last time your name is spoken.

3- seems to be my number.

It's the number of times I repeat something on my way to write it down so I don't forget it, except I sometimes forget where I wrote it.

It's the number of times I check to make sure I locked the doors!

It's the number of times it takes me to remember WHY I CAME IN HERE???

It appears to be the number of times I tell my daughter something ...

"Mom you already told me that twice"...
"well I'm telling you again aren't I"?????

2- Double-checking to see if I did something that is automatic with no thought. Locking the door is an example. You do it automatically. LOL

3- the number of times I had to read the question. Lol

And, this one didn't have a specific number, I have a feeling it changes regularly:

"The number of times I have to rock/pump before I can get off the couch."

What's Your Number?

The Procrastination Club

When we retire, we finally have a lot of time on our hands to do those things we have always wanted.

Some of us dive into that time, more scheduled than they were in their working years, trying to get the most bang for their buck out of the years they have left.

Others are intent on a whole lot of well deserved "Nuttin Honey", having worked for so many years, and feeling just and due downtime and rest.

Then there are those like me- **The Procrastination Club.** I have the best of intentions. I can kill a tree making lists years in advance of things I must accomplish upon retirement.

But, when that time of freedom truly comes, there is a very good chance I will spend a certain amount of time each day perusing Facebook to see who else is on, not getting stuff done.

So I checked in with our lovely Sarcastic Seniors and asked the burning question-

"Should we start a Procrastination Club for Seniors?"

When they got around to answering, it looked like this-

I am a procrastinator too. I would love to join your club. But last weekend, I did file my taxes.

I'm in!

I'll read this later.

Absolutely! Whenever we get around to it.

And hopefully learning something from what others have experienced.

Ah... but.... this is the time set aside for interacting with some of my own species! A rare occurrence and mostly avoided.

So apropos. Should be cleaning...

I'm in! No due's though, OK?

Pre...

I'm still working on not doing yesterday's work.

As Scarlet O'Hara said, "I'll think about it tomorrow".

I'll comment tomorrow.

I used to be apathetic....... But, now I don't really give a damn.

Later.

To Be Young Again?

At one time or another, all of us have wondered what it would be like to go back in time and start over in life. I thinking aging and facing our eventual mortality has us sometimes questioning the choices we have made along the way.

But I am a firm believer that each step of the way, has brought us exactly to the life we were meant to be living, and if we changed one thing, it may fundamentally change who we are.

So, if I were able to wave a magic wand, and send you back to high school, and you could relive your whole adult life, Would you?

Here is what our Sarcastic Seniors had to say-

Knowing that I would spend 4 years in the same school after going to 22 on the way to my freshman year - yes! One year I spent in 3 different schools, 2 schools for many years.

No, I didn't know myself then. I judged myself by everyone else.

The only people who want to go back to HS, are the people who never left it. For them, it was the best four years of their lives. For the rest of us, it was a "lesson" in reality. I started HS as part of the A crowd. After watching the A crowd pick on everyone else, I started picking on them and kicking their butts. My last two years of HS were spent in detention, because of it.

Not high school. But I'd love to be 30 again.

No- I was not part of their clicks and refused to participate in the pettiness and meanness toward each other.

Only if I could keep the knowledge I've gained over the years.

Yes, absolutely! I'd love to have this opportunity! I'd take all the classes needed to go to college so that I could go to college & pursue the occupation I'd desire so much to have had. I knew in 1984 & the age of 30 that I so much wanted to pursue. The only way I could have done this at the time was to go to school at night & my

husband was uncomfortable with this because of the location.

Absolutely...if I had the knowledge, wisdom, courage, strength, and spirituality I have now. To be able to make a positive difference in mine and others' lives.

No way- total bullying time and like some, it was not my only shining moment in time.

Yes, go to college, have a great career, be retiring next year, moving to some quiet tropical place.

I would go back and do most of it differently...

Not a chance. I was a totally different person then.

Only if I could redo knowing what I know now and have the same kids, which would be impossible because I wouldn't have married the same man. So that's a firm no.

Yes, especially if I knew what I know now. I loved high school, but would actually do my work and not skip as much.

Hell no! ...the confusion, the insecurity, the misinformation, the poor self-image, the becoming pregnant (except that child is one of my best friends now).

Oh no! I have been blessed the first go around. Not going to tempt fate!

Yes, would have liked to have 4 years in one high school.

I don't want to relive the pain in my life!

NO! Those were terrible times! Not fitting in, bullying, etc There isn't enough money to pay me to go back.

No. I wouldn't want to be young and starting over in the world we are living in.

I would be more social.

No way in hell! Too many abusers... in every grade.

No, wouldn't want to start all over again.

No, I would not risk not having the family and friends I have now.

No way! It was miserable enough the first time!

No. But I do wish I'd known then what I know now.

No way!! The worst time of my life!

No!! Too much heartbreak! Never want to go back through so much pain at any age! I made it through with the Lord's help, I am truly blessed today!

I would. I'd have my mom and dad and other family. Live in the home I loved. Have many good friends and good times.

I had a great time back then, but go back? No.

Yes, only if I could retain the knowledge that I have now. I would be so much calmer. I wouldn't care who liked me and who didn't. I would go to college right after high school instead of waiting until I was 40.

No, I'm have made it through my life to retirement. I don't think there is anything I want to do over or change. Who would want to go back knowing you need to work 40+ years to retire?

The Games Seniors Play

As I have aged, I have mastered the fine art of being able to laugh at myself. It beats the hell out of crying every time I do something stupid.

Yesterday, there were at least 3 times that I walked into a room, and couldn't remember what I came in there to get. I decided it is a fun game- a kind of "Hide & Seek" with my memory.

I asked our beloved Seniors, what is their favorite Senior Game, and here is what they had to say:

11.30 pm...Oh no, I forgot I stripped the bed this morning, now I have to make it before I can get into it.

Great now that I am down here, how am I going to get to my feet again.

I hold the ultimate high score in Might As Well Go Pee! Wake up in the morning: Might As Well Go Pee! Go near a Bathroom: Might As Well Go Pee! Commercial on TV: Might As Well Go Pee!

Intermission at the theater: Might As Well Go Pee!

I've gotten pretty good at "Why the hell am I up this early", and, "Where the hell did I just put that?"

Where'd I put my glasses?

What is her name? Or his??? I play that often? Or I play " what is the word for that?"

Did I take my pills or not?

I'm a whiz at "What's that word I'm looking for?"

What hurts today?

What's my cell phone number? Mmm... I don't know, I never call myself..it's got a 911 in there somewhere.. my son-in-law picked out the easiest one he thought I would remember..

Did I call to get my pills renewed?

I'm on the highway, an hour into my trip and suddenly, "did I close the garage door?" Do I go back or call the neighbor to check...

Have you seen the thingy? I'm looking for the thingy!

Where are my glasses, pruning shears, gardening gloves...I just had them, dammit!

I only came for milk, how did I end up with four bags of groceries?

Where are my glasses! My head won't tell!

Today it's where is my debit card, so I can shop on Amazon.

What do I need from the store, makes a list. Gets to store, list not in my purse, tries to think of what I need, checks out, then where did I park my car? Wanders around for 20 minutes, finds the car, now can't find keys. Gets home... the list is on the counter...NOTHING I bought is on the list.

I know I put it somewhere.

Oh, What was I going to say? Dammit!

Let me look for my phone while I am talking on it lol

What is in the attic that I haven't touched in 25 years?

What day is it? That's daily. What's that word again? I know it begins with an R... it never begins with an R.

Did I take my meds already?

Opening my mouth to talk and before any words come out, I forgot what I was going to say!

Lisa's Final Thoughts

Well, here we are, at the end of the series. My, we have covered a lot of stuff in the last 3 books. I am so honored to have been a part of this journey with you. I think many important things have come out of this process.

I think we have proven that laughter IS the best medicine. I think if we can share frustrations about the aging process, in a light-hearted way with a group of our peers, we can feel better knowing we are not alone in our struggles.

Some of the comments I have read while putting this book together have caused non-stop uncontrollable laughter, tears, and an overwhelming desire to put on a Depends before continuing.

You are all Rock Stars! I love the way you support each other, and lift each other up when needed. These are people you have never met. Yet, you are there for each other.

I love that we all live different lives, and have different expertise and experience to bring to the table. And yet, we all go through similar things in this aging process.

You have shared ideas on saving money, hobbies, and getting ready for retirement. You have talked about relationship struggles, loss of loved ones, and financial difficulties.

I think the single biggest thing we have proven, is that **WE ARE!**

We are worthy of contributing to society, and not deserving of being dismissed as "too old".

We are useful. Our experiences and wisdom can be of great use to the younger generations, and they would be wise to remember that.

We are the historians of our families.

We are the volunteers that keep things going. As retired people, we make up one of the largest segments of volunteers, as we finally have the time to do it.

We are the heart of our families.

We are the generation that has lived through the most change and innovation- from black and white 3 channel TV, to the internet, we have seen enormous change in our lives.

And**, We are** the secret society- the last ones left able to decipher cursive writing, and do "Old Math".

And, even though this is the last book in the series, our fun together is just beginning. The Sarcastic Seniors are going to be around for a long long time.

I am going to spend the next couple of years working on my first novel. Of course, many giggle breaks with you fine folks will be required...

Thank you all for being the wonderful, wacky, & witty Gems that make me smile every day.

Lisa

Oh, and The Legal Stuff

All of the comments within the book come from the Sarcastic Seniors. But, I will always leave off the contributor's name, to protect their privacy and always allow them to speak freely.

The only folks mentioned by name, are the ones who have given me permission to print their names in the acknowledgment section.

As far as my personal Stories go, names have been changed to protect the innocent, or guilty, depending on the story.

Acknowledgments

We are truly grateful for each of the 47000+ Sarcastic Seniors that have been a part of this journey and an ongoing source of entertainment in our little community.

There are no words to accurately describe my gratitude. Thank you, from the bottom of my heart, and I hope we are laughing together for many years to come.

We also want to specifically acknowledge these contributors, who were brave enough to be mentioned by name:

Debbie Hicks Patt

Daisy Moberley

Willow Kaye

Clara Bates

Carrie Christy

Brenda Key

Marlene McGregory

Deanie Hamilton Berry

Barbara Parker

Donna Henriksen Wallace

Colleen Marvin

Donna Wallace

Sharon M. Babb

Mary Jane Malensek

Jo-Ann Ansaldo

Sharon Krause

Claire Kay

Kathleen Tebbetts Lewis

K Kay Aldun

Anna Boyer

Kathy Blodgett

Lorraine Schmitt

Lois Schmitt

Darrelyn Turner

Rebecca Zdepski

Linda Kurlinski

Kim Pogue

Judi Mccullough Sheldon

Darlene Nichol

Jeff Gitlin

Janice Frerichs

Suzanne Brewer Lucci

Deborah Chaplin

L. Felter

Sharon Stevens-Kuncl

Stephanie Hines

Mary Ellis

Debbie Downs

Julie Hobday

Peggy Jones

Vicki LaRue

Emilene Petrus

Deb Breslow

Joanne Perry

Anita M. Kuminecz

Carolann Bérubé

Ann A. Pelliccio

Joann Jenkins

Robyn-Ann Chasse

Bonnie McIsaac

Lois Wollenman

R John Welton

Gloria Berngard

Ellen Rick

J Lynn Marquardt Lesniak

Shirley D'Amico

Kathy Chadwick Dyess

Wendy Gill

Margaret (Peggy) Freshwater

Sammie Maas

Melissa Cabrera

Suzanne Hartwig

Shirley D'Amico

Elaine Rector

Renee Miller

Cathy Lee Rakers

Galen Donovan

Debbie Reynolds

Sandi Wilson

Iris Smith

Made in the USA
Monee, IL
15 August 2020

37287502R00069